WETLANDS

A TRUE BOOK

by
Darlene R. Stille

Children's Press®
A Division of Grolier Publishing
New York London Hong Kong Sydney
Danbury, Connecticut

Water lilies often grow
in freshwater marshes.

Reading Consultant
Linda Cornwell
Coordinator of School Quality
and Professional Improvement
Indiana State Teachers
Association

Content Consultant
Jan Jenner, Ph.D.

Author's Dedication
For Cynthia A. Marquard,
who showed me some of the
world's great ecosystems

The photo on the cover shows
a marsh in Superior National
Forest in Boundary Waters,
Minnesota. The photo on the
title page shows a bog in
Davis, West Virginia.

Visit Children's Press® on the
Internet at:
http://publishing.grolier.com

Library of Congress Cataloging-in-Publication Data

Stille, Darlene R.
    Wetlands / by Darlene R. Stille.
        p.   cm. — (A true book)
    Includes bibliographical references and index.
    Summary: Examines the different types of wetlands and the plant and
animal life they support.
    ISBN: 0-516-21512-4 (lib. bdg.)   0-516-26791-4 (pbk.)
    1. Wetlands—Juvenile literature. [1. Wetlands.] I. Title. II. Series.
QH87.3.S758   1999
578.768—dc21   98-49729
                                                                          CIP
                                                                          AC

GROLIER
PUBLISHING

Contents

What Is a Wetland?   5

Marshes, Swamps, and Bogs   8

Special Wetland Plants   22

Wetland Animals   26

Wetlands and Our Water   32

Saving Wetlands   38

To Find Out More   44

Important Words   46

Index   47

Meet the Author   48

Suckerbrook Swamp
in Pennsylvania

What Is a Wetland?

A wetland is land that is underwater for at least part of the year. Some wetlands are very large, but others are as small as a backyard.

The water in wetlands can come from rain or melting snow. It can also come from underground water. It can even come from rivers and streams or from the ocean.

There are many different kinds of wetlands. Wetlands called prairie potholes form on the midwestern plains.

Prairie potholes often form on grasslands in the midwestern United States.

Sloughs often form along the banks of slow-moving rivers and streams.

Wetlands called sloughs (SLEWS) form along lakes and rivers. But the three best-known kinds of wetlands are marshes, swamps, and bogs.

Marshes, Swamps, and Bogs

Marshes have a shallow layer of water almost all the time. A marsh is so wet that trees cannot grow there. Grassy plants like cattails, bulrushes, sedges, and reeds are found in marshes. Water lilies and duckweed often grow on top of the water.

This swamp is covered with water plants. Cattails and other grasses grow along the water's edge.

A saltwater marsh on
Deal Island in Maryland

Most marshes hold fresh water. Freshwater marshes are often found along the shores of lakes or rivers. But saltwater marshes sometimes form in places where a river flows into the ocean. The water level in a saltwater marsh rises and falls with the ocean's tides.

Some parts of a swamp are underwater all year round. But other parts are not always flooded. Because the land in

a swamp is a little drier than the land in a marsh, some trees and shrubs can grow in swamps.

Oak and maple trees can grow only in swamps that are not always flooded. Strange-looking trees called bald cypresses grow in

Bald cypress trees may be up to 100 feet (30 meters) tall.

swamps in the southern part of the United States. They can grow tall and strong even though the swamps they live in are covered with water most of the time. Mangrove trees grow in saltwater swamps found in warm places. Most trees need fresh water to grow, but mangroves grow well in salt water.

Trees are not the only plants that live in swamps. Vines twist around the tree trunks, and

A mangrove tree's tangled roots reach far above the water's surface.

Spanish moss hangs from a cypress tree growing in a Louisiana swamp.

mosses grow on the tree bark. A plant called Spanish moss often hangs from the limbs of bald cypress trees.

Bogs are found in cool parts of the world. In the United States, there are large bogs in Maine, Minnesota, and Alaska.

This bog is located in Manistee National Forest in Michigan.

Hungry Plants

Believe it or not, some bog plants eat meat! They trap insects for food. The sundew plant catches insects in its sticky leaves.

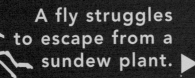

A fly struggles to escape from a sundew plant. ▶

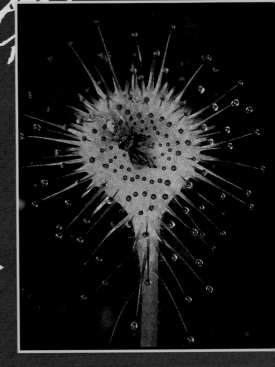

The pitcher plant has a long tube that fills with water. Insects that go into this tube drown.

◀ Many insects drown in water that collects inside pitcher plants.

Bogs are also common in Canada and northern Europe. All of the water in a bog comes from rain or melted snow. Very few plants grow in bogs because the damp, spongy soil does not have many nutrients.

Peat moss is the most common plant found in bogs. Peat moss grows in bunches on the top of a bog. When peat moss and other bog plants die, they lie on top of the bog like a

After this peat has dried out, people on the Shetland Islands in Scotland will use it to heat their homes.

huge mat. This mat of dead plants is called peat. In Ireland and other countries in northern Europe, people dry the peat and burn it like wood to heat their homes.

Some bogs are used to grow foods that we eat. Farmers on Cape Cod, Massachusetts, grow cranberries in bogs.

Cranberries are grown in bogs.

Special Wetland Plants

Oxygen is an important gas in the air we breathe. Without oxygen, we would die. Plants need oxygen too. They use their roots to get oxygen from the soil.

Soil covered with water is low in oxygen, so wetland

The bulging "knees" on these bald cypress trees collect oxygen and help keep the trees steady.

plants have special ways of getting oxygen. Bald cypress trees have "knees" on their roots that stick up above the

23

water in a swamp. The knees also help hold the tree steady in the muddy soil. Other plants have roots that stick up above the water.

Some wetland plants have hollow stems that carry oxygen from their leaves to their roots. The hollow stems of bulrushes are so large that a person can use them like a tube to breathe underwater.

These bulrushes
have hollow stems.

Wetland Animals

Many kinds of animals live in wetlands. Wetlands have mosquitoes, dragonflies, beetles, butterflies, and thousands of other insects.

Fish and amphibians, such as frogs and salamanders, are found in most marshes and swamps. Amphibians spend

A bullfrog (left) waits for prey in Great Swamp in New Jersey. A red bellied turtle (right) basks in the sun at Everglades National Park in Florida.

part of their life in the water and part on land.

Some wetlands have snakes, turtles, and other reptiles. Alligators live in swamps in warm parts of the world.

A brown lemming hides among grasses in a bog in Alaska.

Many types of mammals live in wetlands too. Swamps are home to deer, bears, and rabbits. Muskrats and beavers live in marshes. Bog lemmings are rat-like mammals that live in bogs.

Wetlands are also very important for birds. Some birds spend their whole life at one wetland. Egrets, cormorants,

A snowy egret and two double-crested cormorants perch on a mangrove tree in Ding Darling National Wildlife Refuge near Sanibel Island, Florida.

flamingos, herons, and pelicans live in swamps in the southern United States all year round.

Many kinds of birds do not stay in one place the whole year. Many ducks and geese fly thousands of miles every year. In the fall, they travel south to warmer places. In the spring, they fly north to their summer home. When these birds get tired or hungry, they rest at wetlands.

These six geese are flying away from a wetland in Louisiana.

Wetlands and Our Water

Wetlands are very important to people, too. The water in some wetlands sinks down into the ground. When people dig wells, they are looking for this groundwater. Many people drink groundwater, and farmers use it to water their crops.

The water sprayed from these irrigation trucks came from Everglades National Park, a huge wetland in Florida.

Wetlands help make water pure. The soil and plants in wetlands can remove dangerous

Many wetland plants and the soil they grow in remove pollutants from the water.

materials called pollutants from water. The pollutants may come from factories, mines, fertilizers, or even acid rain. Tiny wetland bacteria destroy some pollutants, too. When water leaves a wetland, it is much cleaner than when it entered.

Wetlands also help control flooding. When a river overflows its banks, wetlands act like big sponges. They soak up a lot of the extra water.

The Everglades

ALABAMA
GEORGIA

Atlantic Ocean

FLORIDA

Gulf of Mexico

0   200 miles
0   300 kilometers

Lake Okeechobee

Everglades

Miami

EVERGLADES NATIONAL PARK

Florida Bay

FLORIDA

CUBA

The Everglades is one of the largest wetlands in the United States. It is in southern Florida.

This area has many swamps and marshes. It is home to many kinds of plants and animals. Many people in Florida get their drinking water from the

Air plants called bromeliads grow on the trunks of some trees in Everglades National Park.

Everglades. The water is also used on farms, so sometimes the water level in the Everglades is too low. When this happens, engineers pump water into the Everglades.

Saving Wetlands

For many years, people did not know how important wetlands are. They thought it would be better to drain off the water and use the land to grow crops or build homes. During the 1700s and 1800s, settlers in the American West drained more than half the

Early pioneers often drained wetland waters, so they could plant crops and build homes.

wetlands in the United States.

Today, we know that we must save our wetlands. They supply us with safe water to drink and help prevent flooding. They are the home of many endangered plants and animals. Wetlands may even be important for keeping temperatures on Earth just right for people.

Some scientists think our planet is growing warmer

Wetlands can be beautiful, but they also prevent flooding and remove pollutants from water.

Wetland plants may remove large quantities of carbon dioxide from the air. We might not be able to survive without them.

because the air has more carbon dioxide in it all the time. Carbon dioxide is a gas given off when we burn coal, oil, peat, or natural gas. Wetland plants may remove carbon dioxide from the air, so saving wetlands might help us save ourselves.

To Find Out More

Here are some additional resources to help you learn more about wetlands:

 **Books**

Collard, Sneed B. **Our Wet World.** Charlesbridge Publishing, 1998.

Field, Mary, Margaret J. Anderson, Karen F. Stephenson, and Michael Maydak. **Leapfrogging Through Wetlands.** Dog-Eared Publications, 1999.

Fowler, Allen. **Life in a Wetland.** Children's Press, 1998.

Freeman, Marcia. **Wetlands: Big Book.** Newbridge Communications, 1998.

_____. **Wetlands: Student Book.** Newbridge Communications. 1998.

Leon, Vicki. **Wetlands: All About Bogs, Bayous, Swamps, Sloughs, and a Salt Marsh or Two.** Silver Burdett, 1998.

Pipes, Rose. **Wetlands.** Raintree Steck-Vaughn Publishers, 1998.

Organizations and Online Sites

Conflict in the Wetlands
http://www3.ask.net/ ~aceacad/thinkquest/ray/ index.html

This site was created by students. It gives other young people ideas about what they can do to save wetlands.

Lost Wetlands
http://seawifs.gsfc.nasa.gov /OCEAN_PLANET/HTML/ peril_wetlands.html

Find out why it is important to save wetlands.

National Wetlands Research Center
http://www.nwrc.nbs.gov/

This site has plenty of information about the plants and animals that live in or around wetlands. You will also find fun activities.

Wetlands International
http://www.wetlands. agro.nl/

Learn about efforts to save wetlands in Africa, Europe, and the Middle East.

Important Words

amphibian an animal that spends part of its life on land and part in the water

bacteria tiny living things that can only be seen with a microscope

bog a wetland in a cool place, plants in a bog build up over time and form peat

mammal an animal that has a backbone and feeds its young with mother's milk

marsh a wetland that is covered with water most of the time and has no trees

pollutant any material that can damage living things or their environment

reptile an animal that lives on land, lays eggs, and is cold-blooded

soil the dirt and other materials that make up the top layer of earth

swamp a wetland that dries up for part of the year and has trees

Index

(**Boldface** page numbers
indicate illustrations.)

amphibians, 26–27, **27,** 46
bacteria, wetland, 35, 46
bald cypress trees,
    13–14, **13,** 16, **16,**
    23–24, **23**
birds, 29-30, **29, 31**
bogs, **2,** 7, 17–21, **17,**
    21, 28, 46
carbon dioxide, 41–43
cranberries, 21, **21**
Ding Darling National
    Wildlife Refuge, **29**
draining of wetlands,
    38–43, **39**
Everglades, 27, 33,
    36–37, **36, 37**
flooding, 11, 13–15, 35,
    40–41
groundwater, 5, 32–33,
    33, 36–37, 40

insects, 18, 26
mammals, 28, **28,** 46
mangrove trees, 14, **15,**
    29
marshes, **1, 2,** 7–8, **10,**
    11, 26–28, 36, 46
oxygen, 22–24
peat, 20, **20,** 43
peat moss, 19–20, **20,** 43
plants, 8, **9,** 14–16, **16,**
    18–24, **18, 20, 21, 25,**
    34, 36–37, **37,** 40, **42**
pollutants, 33–35, **34,**
    41, 46
prairie potholes, 6, **6**
reptiles, 27, 46
saving of wetlands,
    38–43
sloughs, 7, **7**
soil, 12, 33, **34,** 46
swamps, 4, 7, **9,** 11–16,
    12, 16, 23–30, 36, 46
wetland, defined, 5

Meet the Author

Darlene R. Stille lives in Chicago, Illinois, and is executive editor of the World Book Annuals and World Book's Online Service. She has written many books for Children's Press, including *Extraordinary Women Scientists*, *Extraordinary Women of Medicine*, four True Books about the human body, and four other True Books about ecosystems.

Photographs ©: Corbis-Bettmann: 39; Jonathan Nutt: 13, 16, 31; Peter Arnold Inc.: cover (Peter Arnold), 20 (John Cancalosi), 37 (Patricia Caulfield), 25 (Walter H. Hodge), 2 (Jan-Peter Laball), 27 right (Fritz Polking), 29 (Ed Reschke), 15 (Kevin Schafer); Photo Researchers: 7 (John Bova), 23 (Patricia Caulfield), 27 left (E. R. Degginger), 34 (B. Derig), 41 (Douglas Faulkner), 4, 9, 42 (Michael P. Gadomski), 33 (Tom & Pat Leeson), 1 (D. Lyons), 28 (Tom McHugh), 10 (Robert Noonan); Visuals Unlimited: 12 (Bill Beatty), 21 (John D. Cunningham), 18 top (Robert W. Domm), 17 (Ross Frid), 18 bottom (John Gerlach), 6 (Kirtley-Perkins).

Map by Joe LeMonnier.